New
Covenant
Realities

New Covenant Realities

A Journey to

True Freedom in Christ

by

Pastor Brian A. J. Bourque

New Covenant Realities
A Journey to True Freedom in Christ
First Edition January 2025
By Brian A.J. Bourque
Copyright 2025
All rights Reserved-Standard Copyright License

Unless otherwise noted, all scripture quotations
are from the King James Version of the Bible.

9 781300 757238

Dedication

I dedicate this book to the memory of my wonderful mom, Sara Bourque, for she was always a constant in my life. She was one of my biggest supporters as I pursued a life in ministry. Her love, support and prayers have always been there for me!

Foreward

I have known Pastor Brian Bourque for about five years and many times I have heard him speak in Pentecostal and Victory churches as well as home church settings with a variety of denominations represented. In all cases Brian has shown a passion for, and deep knowledge of the Word of God and the power of prayer.

Having seen miraculous examples of divine healing in his own life, he often leads his listeners into deeper faith and trust in the healing nature of God's character.

In his writing about the realities of the new covenant through the sacrifice of Jesus Christ, Brian has shared personal examples, as well as scriptural truth, all of which will inspire readers to turn to the scriptures for further insight and revelation.

Please read this book and be on the lookout for future publications as Brian continues to share his faith, his experiences and his relationship with Jesus.

David Mulford
Stony Plain Alberta
January 2025

Contents

Chapter 1

Jesus Made an End to the Law and to the Curse

Many times, I think we read the Bible as a book of promises, a book of history, or just a book of experiences that people had with the presence of God. In a time of prayer that I was having with God, this came to my mind, and into my heart; that the Bible is in many ways, those things, but I believe that scripture and the Bible is also, a book of covenants. If we don't experience the covenants of God, the way they were intended for us to experience them, we will miss out on the things that God has planned and purposed for our lives. We can't be living a Covenant Christian Life unless we have a New Covenant Reality. One of the things that I believe we need to understand is that Jesus made an end to the law. **2 Corinthians chapter 3:6-18** says: *6 who also made us sufficient as ministers of the new covenant, not of the letter but of the Spirit; for the letter kills, but the Spirit gives life.*

Glory of the New Covenant

7 But if the ministry of death, written and engraved on stones, was glorious, so that the children of Israel could

2

not look steadily at the face of Moses because of the glory of his countenance, which glory was passing away, 8 how will the ministry of the Spirit not be more glorious? 9 For if the ministry of condemnation had glory, the ministry of righteousness exceeds much more in glory. 10 For even what was made glorious had no glory in this respect, because of the glory that excels. 11 For if what is passing away was glorious, what remains is much more glorious.12 Therefore, since we have such hope, we use great boldness of speech— 13 unlike Moses, who put a veil over his face so that the children of Israel could not look steadily at the end of what was passing away. 14 But their minds were blinded. For until this day the same veil remains unlifted in the reading of the Old Testament, because the veil is taken away in Christ. 15 But even to this day, when Moses is read, a veil lies on their heart. 16 Nevertheless when one turns to the Lord, the veil is taken away. 17 Now the Lord is the Spirit; and where the Spirit of the Lord is, there is liberty. 18 But we all, with unveiled face, beholding as in a mirror the glory of the Lord, are being transformed into the same image from glory to glory, just as by the Spirit of the Lord.

When you read the scripture, you can see many different things. There are things that believers need to realize, about the letter of the law, that to continually try to live a Christian life under the law is death. In my experience as a pastor, I've seen so much of the church, condemning themselves, and each other with the law. They use the law as a measuring stick, measuring one another to see if they are good enough, or even qualified, to receive anything from God. There is no life in the law. All that you will find in the law is death and condemnation. The law continually reminds us that we're never going to be good enough to be able to receive what God has for our lives. All it ends up doing is killing our faith and our belief in God, portraying God as judge and not as a father. However, when we operate in the spirit of God and the outflowing of his love, we understand that his desire for us is to walk in liberty, with life walked in freedom.

There's a big difference between the operation of the law and the operation of the grace of God. When we serve God under the law, we serve out of fear of being cursed. You know, most of my Christian life that has been the case. I had to do so many different things and had to be able to behave a certain way to make sure that I wouldn't end up causing myself to be cursed.

Do you know what the one who curses is? He is the enemy, the devil. God did not come to curse; God came to set us free. I don't want to serve God out of fear; I want to serve him with a free and overflowing heart to experience relationship with him, and to be filled with his presence. When we serve God out of rules and regulations, that if we don't do this, or we don't do that, that God is going to punish us and bring evil upon us, fear fills our relationship with Him. It almost sounds like it portrays God as a bully, but we can't serve God out of fear; we must serve Him out of relationship.

I have repeatedly said that the law will always make you a servant, but grace will make you a son or daughter who serves in the new covenant. We serve God out of love, because he has accepted us and forgiven us of our sins. The new covenant reality is that we don't serve him because we have to; we serve him because we want to, and that makes a big difference in having a relationship with God.

This reminds me of a request that I received while I was pastoring a small church in a tiny community of Nova Scotia called Bible Hill. While I was there, a young lady had been diagnosed with leukemia. I was asked to go and pray for her, and so I decided that I should go. During that time, I was in prayer and asking the Lord how I was going to be able to minister life to her and how I was going to be able to minister healing to her physical body. I remember the Lord speaking to my heart and saying, "I don't want you to pray for her unless she asks you to pray." So, I went to visit her at the hospital. The first day she didn't ask me to pray. We talked about everything under the sun, just making small talk. I went back the next day, and repeatedly for a period of almost two weeks the same thing happened. I remember at the end of the two weeks I was in her hospital room with her, and we were just chatting, and she said to me, "You know, I said to my dad that the minister is going to come in the first day, and he's going to pray for me and I'm never going to see him again. I was so happy that you didn't ask to pray for me and that you came back the next day and the following day." She said, "What you don't know is that in my heart I had already talked to the Lord telling Him that if you came in, and just did your routine and went home and if I never saw you again, I would know that the Lord isn't real!"

She had made a list of many different questions she had about the Lord, and every time I went to the hospital, we talked about those questions. She told me that after that she was able to cross off some of these questions from her list, until every question that she had of the Lord was answered. What an amazing experience! At the end, after all her questions were answered, she said,
 "I'm going to ask you to pray for me, but I don't believe I'll be healed. I don't deserve to be healed."

I'll never forget that day. The thought that came through my heart and my mind as I replied to her was how awesome it was that none of us get what we deserve when we receive what Jesus has purchased for us. I believe it was Paul the apostle who said that we all have sinned and fallen short of the glory of God. He said that none of us will ever be perfect enough or deserve anything from God. That is the beauty of the plan of redemption for our lives.

That day I remember laying my hands on her and praying. It was many people praying, not just my prayers. Her parents were praying, the church was praying, and her friends were praying. Many different people were praying for her, so I'm not saying that it was my prayer that changed anything, but I will say it was the presence of Jesus that changed everything. I do remember praying, and it was only a few days later that she called me and told me that the leukemia had gone into remission. She was so excited and remained in remission until it came to the point when they were wanting to do a bone marrow transplant in her physical body. Her sister was going to be the one to donate that bone marrow but as her sister went to the hospital to get checked over to see if she would be a match, for her to be able to receive the transplant the doctors told her that she had *almost* everything that she needed. However, the final test would not line up and I remember the young lady calling me back on the phone, sounding a little bit discouraged.

She said to me, "I can't get the bone marrow transplant. I don't know what's going to happen." I remember my reply to her was, "Your sister is not getting the glory for this, but Jesus is, so let's pray!"

So, we prayed again and believed that God would just move and intervene on her behalf, that the presence of God would simply touch her physical body and that she would be healed. I remember that moment when I finished that prayer, that there was something tangible about God's presence that was flowing over her life, and I knew in my spirit that everything was going to be OK.

It was a few weeks later that I received a call from her again and she was so excited she was nearly screaming to me on the phone, and she said, "Pastor Brian you'll never guess what happened!" and I asked her to please tell me. She said, "The doctors have no explanation for it, but there is a gene that came into my bloodstream that is producing marrow in my bones. They don't even have a name for it!" I remember telling her that I had a name for it. I told her we would call it the "God Gene"! Suddenly, the experience of God had brought healing to this young lady's body, but not because she deserved it. Out of her own mouth she says, "We can pray, but I don't deserve to be healed and that is the same thing for all of us. None of us deserve anything, but we don't get what we deserve. We get what Jesus bought.

That is why I am convinced that the ministry of the law is done away with. According to the scripture we are no longer under the law. We are under the ministry of the Spirit, and that is why it's so important that we operate our lives after the things of the Spirit of God, and not after our flesh. Our battle is always spiritual, and as **Ephesians Chapter 6, verse 12** says; *12 For we do not wrestle against flesh and blood, but against principalities, against powers, against the rulers of the darkness of this age, against spiritual hosts of wickedness in the heavenly places.*
I thank God that in the middle of these battles, and what we wrestle against, the veil has been taken away, and there's nothing that separates me from the love of God.

This reminds me of the scripture in **John Chapter 3, verse 16 and 17** where we read: *16 For God so loved the world that He gave His only begotten Son, that whoever believes in Him should not perish but have everlasting life.* It doesn't say that God loves perfect people. It says that God so loved *the world* that he gave his only begotten son, that whoever believes in him would not perish, but have everlasting life. So, we're not saved based upon our behavior modification. We are saved, because we believe in Jesus, and because believing in Jesus brings salvation into our lives. I also love verse 17. It says: *17 For God did not send His Son into the world to condemn the world, but that the world through Him might be saved.*

I believe Jesus didn't come to point a finger at everyone's sin and shortcomings. I believe that He came to save us from our shortcomings and save us from our sins. I also believe his love for us will not be separated from us. In the book of **Romans Chapter 8 verses 35-39** it says, *35 Who shall separate us from the love of Christ? Shall tribulation, or distress, or persecution, or famine, or nakedness, or peril, or sword? 36 As it is written: "For Your sake we are killed all day long; We are accounted as sheep for the slaughter." 37 Yet in all these things we are more than conquerors through Him who loved us. 38 For I am persuaded that neither death nor life, nor angels nor principalities nor powers, nor things present nor things to come, 39 nor height nor depth, nor any other created thing, shall be able to separate us from the love of God which is in Christ Jesus our Lord.*

I believe with all my heart that we cannot be separated from the love of Christ. I believe that Christ made up his mind when he decided to go to the cross of Calvary, that he was just going to love us. I believe that his love cannot be separated from us, but I believe we can separate our love from him.

Notes

Chapter 2

Christ Redeemed Us From the Curse of the Law

In this chapter, I want to look at whether Christ desired for us to live by the law and be cursed by the law. Why would he redeem us from the curse of the law?
Galations 3:13-25 says *this ¹³ Christ has redeemed us from the curse of the law, having become a curse for us (for it is written, "Cursed is everyone who hangs on a tree"), ¹⁴ that the blessing of Abraham might come upon the Gentiles in Christ Jesus, that we might receive the promise of the Spirit through faith.*

The Changeless Promise

¹⁵ Brethren, I speak in the manner of men: Though it is only a man's covenant, yet if it is confirmed, no one annuls or adds to it. ¹⁶ Now to Abraham and his Seed were the promises made. He does not say, "And to seeds," as of many, but as of one, "And to your Seed," who is Christ. ¹⁷ And this I say, that the law, which was four hundred and thirty years later, cannot annul the covenant that was confirmed before by God in Christ, that it should make the promise of no effect. ¹⁸ For if the inheritance is of the law, it is no longer of promise; but God gave it to Abraham by promise.

Purpose of the Law

¹⁹ What purpose then does the law serve? It was added because of transgressions, till the Seed should come ...

I want to stop right there and just add some clarity. The law was there until the seed should come, but after the seed has come, we need to look at this because some people still think, for some reason, that they are under the law. We are not under the law; we are under Christ. We are under His Spirit and His anointing. His way of doing things is so powerful, and if we can grasp that, we'll be able to live a life of victory in every area of our lives.

The law came because of transgressions. When I look at the Old Testament and I read the book of Genesis, I see that Methuselah lived nine hundred and sixty-nine years. Then we see that Noah built the ark, and I believe that Methuselah was still alive while Noah was building the ark. If there was no law, there would be no penalty for sin, and then, if there was no penalty for sin, there would be no death. That is why people were living such a long life.

Can you imagine living nine hundred and sixty-nine years? That's a long time, and I believe that the law was an act of grace. God's desire was that humanity would not live in the perpetual state of sin year after year after year, without being redeemed, in fellowship, and in relationship with Him. Thank God, the law was done away with when the seed had come, glory to God! If that doesn't make you happy, nothing will!

As we keep reading in **Galatians 3, at verse 19** *What purpose then does the law serve? It was added because of transgressions, till the Seed should come to whom the promise was made; and it was appointed through angels by the hand of a mediator. ²⁰ Now a mediator does not mediate for one only, but God is one.²¹ Is the law then against the promises of God? Certainly not! For if there had been a law given which could have given life, truly righteousness would have been by the law. ²² But the Scripture has confined all under sin, that the promise by faith in Jesus Christ might be given to those who believe.*

So here we see that the law had an inability to be able to give life to the believer. If there had been a way that the law could have brought life to us, then Jesus would never have had to die. The promise is not given to us because we have everything right in our lives, the promise is given to us because we believe. That is the power of being a believer in the body of Christ. In my own life, my own Christianity, as a pastor I will tell you many times that I am not perfect in any way, but I know one thing; I know that Jesus loves me, and that no matter what happens in my life, I can believe in Jesus to be saved.

Continuing in Galatians it says, *23 But before faith came, we were kept under guard by the law, kept for the faith which would afterward be revealed. 24 Therefore the law was our tutor to bring us to Christ, that we might be justified by faith. 25 But after faith has come, we are no longer under a tutor....*

I think we need to stop there for a moment and begin to look at this. The law was there to bring us to Christ. If there was no law, we would not know what's right and what's wrong. The law gives you boundaries in your life concerning what we should, and should not do, but the law cannot empower you to live right. The law was made to condemn you when you did wrong, so Jesus did not just come to show you the law, He came to redeem you from its curse, in order that he could empower you to live a victorious Christian life. The law was a schoolmaster to bring us under Christ, that we might be justified by faith, and after faith is come, we are no longer under the schoolmaster or the law.

We must understand that we are not under the law, but we are under faith. God does not want us to serve him by the law. He wants us to serve him through faith. There are many sins out there that could cause us all to point fingers at many other people, and even point the fingers at ourselves, but I think one of the greatest sins in the body of Christ is that which scripture says is "anything that is not faith". We need to be in faith, so we don't live in sin.

We can't change our lives by trying to change our behavior. We need to have faith in God, for him to change our behavior. The one thing I love about the grace of God is that grace leaves the door open for me to continually come to the presence of God in order that I might be changed. In **Galatians chapter 4, verses 21 to 31** it says; *21 Tell me, you who desire to be under the law, do you not hear the law? 22 For it is written that Abraham had two sons: the one by a bondwoman, the other by a freewoman. 23 But he who was of the bondwoman was born according to the flesh, and he of the freewoman through promise, 24 which things are symbolic. For these are [a]the two covenants: the one from Mount Sinai which gives birth to bondage, which is Hagar— 25 for this Hagar is Mount Sinai in Arabia, and corresponds to Jerusalem which now is, and is in bondage with her children— 26 but the Jerusalem above is free, which is the mother of us all. 27 For it is written:*

"Rejoice, O barren,
You who do not bear!
Break forth and shout,
You who are not in labor!
For the desolate has many more children
Than she who has a husband."
28 Now we, brethren, as Isaac was, are children of promise. 29 But, as he who was born according to the flesh then persecuted him who was born according to the Spirit, even so it is now. 30 Nevertheless what does the

Scripture say? "Cast out the bondwoman and her son, for the son of the bondwoman shall not be heir with the son of the freewoman." ³¹ So then, brethren, we are not children of the bondwoman but of the free.

When I look at this, I see that we are like Isaac. We are children of promise. That's why Abraham's blessings are mine, because I'm born of promise, not of the law. Here it talks about casting out the bondwoman, or the law which leads to bondage, but the promise leads to freedom. All the law is ever going to do, if we keep rehearsing in our lives repeatedly, is lead us to bondage. If we look at everything that we do, and feel we need to qualify to be good enough to get into the presence of God, it will lead us to stop pursuing His presence. The law is always a measurement to see if we are good enough! I believe that scripture has concluded that we will never be good enough, but Jesus is good enough for us to be able to enter His presence by grace.

It is the grace of God that gives us the ability to go into God's presence over and over again. I don't think it matters what we've ever done in our lives, that we should ever stop going into the presence of God. We should never stop pursuing God. We should never stop praying to God, and reading God's Word, because of things we've done in our lives. We need to continue, no matter what we've done in our lives because we cannot change ourselves. We cannot qualify ourselves.

We have been qualified by the blood of Jesus, and by His sacrifice on the cross at Calvary. I hope this helps you because I think this is a big area in many Christians' lives that prevents them from living a life of Victory.

Notes

Chapter 3

The Priesthood Has Changed

The concept of priesthood has been a central element in various religious traditions throughout history. In the Christian faith, the role of the priest has evolved significantly over time, as depicted in the New Testament book of Hebrews. This book explores the transformation of the priesthood as described in **Hebrews 7:11-28, Hebrews 8:6-13, Hebrews 9:1-28,** and **Hebrews 10:1-39**, highlighting the shift from the Old Covenant priesthood to the New Covenant priesthood established through Jesus Christ.

The priesthood has undergone a profound transformation in Christian theology, as evidenced in the Book of Hebrews. Drawing upon the rich tapestry of Old Testament imagery and symbolism, Hebrews presents a compelling case for the supremacy and sufficiency of Christ as the ultimate high priest. Through a close examination of select passages in Hebrews, we can discern the dynamic evolution of the priesthood and its significance for believers:

From the book of **Hebrews chapter 7, verses 11-28**
we read; *11. If therefore perfection were by the Levitical
priesthood, (for under it the people received the law),
what further need was there that another priest should
rise after the order of Melchisedec, and not be called after
the order of Aaron? 12. For the priesthood being changed,
there is made of necessity a change also of the law. 13. For
he of whom these things are spoken pertaineth to another
tribe, of which no man gave attendance at the altar.
14. For it is evident that our Lord sprang out of Juda; of
which tribe Moses spake nothing concerning priesthood.
15. And it is yet far more evident: for that after the
similitude of Melchisedec there ariseth another priest,
16. Who is made, not after the law of a carnal
commandment, but after the power of an endless life.
17. For he testifieth, Thou art a priest for ever after the
order of Melchisedec. 18. For there is verily a disannulling
of the commandment going before for the weakness and
unprofitableness thereof. 19. For the law made nothing
perfect, but the bringing in of a better hope did; by the
which we draw nigh unto God. 20. And inasmuch as not
without an oath he was made priest: 21. (For those priests
were made without an oath; but this with an oath by him
that said unto him, The Lord sware and will not repent,
Thou art a priest for ever after the order of Melchisedec:)
22. By so much was Jesus made a surety of a better
testament. 23. And they truly were many priests, because
they were not suffered to continue by reason of death: 24.
But this man, because he continueth ever, hath an*

unchangeable priesthood. 25. Wherefore he is able also to save them to the uttermost that come unto God by him, seeing he ever liveth to make intercession for them. 26. For such an high priest became us, who is holy, harmless, undefiled, separate from sinners, and made higher than the heavens; 27. Who needeth not daily, as those high priests, to offer up sacrifice, first for his own sins, and then for the people's: for this he did once, when he offered up himself. 28. For the law maketh men high priests which have infirmity; but the word of the oath, which was since the law, maketh the Son, who is consecrated for evermore.

In **Hebrews 7:11-28**, the author contrasts the Levitical priesthood established under the Old Covenant with the priesthood of Jesus Christ. The Levitical priests were appointed based on genealogy and performed rituals that offered temporary atonement for sins and required continual sacrifices to atone for sin. In contrast, Jesus, as the eternal high priest in the order of Melchizedek, offers a perfect and once-for-all sacrifice through his own blood. This new priesthood transcends the limitations of the old system and is characterized by its permanence, effectiveness, and ability to bring believers into a closer relationship with God, providing complete forgiveness of sins.

Perfection could not be obtained by the Law. Jesus did not come from the priesthood of Aaron or of the Law, He came from the tribe of Judah, from the tribe of Praise and Worship.

God wants our praise more than our sacrifice. That is why what we do for God out of Praise is greater than our sacrifice. We can sacrifice out of the Law because we have to, but God wants us to serve him out of Love and Praise, not because we have to, but because we want to.

I don't have to, I get to, out of my own will and desire to serve and praise God with all my heart. This way we serve God out of faith and not out of fear of breaking the Law. Having said that, what comes to mind is that the law was already broken by every person that was trying to follow it. That is why the law had to be replaced with grace. I believe God wants us to have a faith-filled relationship with him out of grace, instead of a fear-filled relationship with him out of the law.

Faith is a journey; the Law is a grave.

Hebrews 8:6-13 tells us:

6. But now hath he obtained a more excellent ministry, by how much also he is the mediator of a better covenant, which was established upon better promises. 7. For if that first covenant had been faultless, then should no place have been sought for the second. 8. For finding fault with them, he saith, Behold, the days come, saith the Lord, when I will make a new covenant with the house of Israel and with the house of Judah: 9. Not according to the covenant that I made with their fathers in the day when I took them by the hand to lead them out of the land of Egypt; because they continued not in my covenant, and I regarded them not, saith the Lord. 10. For this is the covenant that I will make with the house of Israel after those days, saith the Lord; I will put my laws into their mind, and write them in their hearts: and I will be to them a God, and they shall be to me a people: 11. And they shall not teach every man his neighbour, and every man his brother, saying, Know the Lord: for all shall know me, from the least to the greatest. 12. For I will be merciful to their unrighteousness, and their sins and their iniquities will I remember no more. 13. In that he saith, A new covenant, he hath made the first old. Now that which decayeth and waxeth old is ready to vanish away.

Hebrews 8:6-13: The author of Hebrews continues to highlight the superiority of the New Covenant established by Christ over the Old Covenant. Under the New Covenant, Jesus serves as the mediator of a better covenant based on better promises. This new covenant reality is not based on external regulations and rituals but on the internal transformation of the heart. Through the work of Christ, believers have direct access to God's presence and experience forgiveness of sins along with reconciliation and relationship with Him.

Hebrews 8:6-13: Building upon the foundation laid out in Hebrews 7, the author expounds on the superiority of the New Covenant inaugurated by Christ. The New Covenant is founded on better promises and mediated by Jesus as the high priest who intercedes on behalf of believers. Unlike the Old Covenant, which relied on external rituals and regulations having to measure up to a certain standard of living, but the New Covenant brings about an internal transformation of the heart, offering believers direct access to God's presence and the assurance of salvation through faith in Christ.

Through this passage we can be so very thankful that we serve a God who loves us so much that He himself has become our mediator and stands in the gap for us.
Many times, I have been asked the question why I believe in Christianity. For me it's very simple. In all the other religions in the world, their Gods always require sacrifice for salvation, but in Christianity we have the only God who sacrifices for our salvation! That statement is true, and I love Him because he first loved me.

Chapter 9 of Hebrews reads as follows; *1. Then verily the first covenant had also ordinances of divine service, and a worldly sanctuary. 2. For there was a tabernacle made; the first, wherein was the candlestick, and the table, and the shewbread; which is called the sanctuary. 3. And after the second veil, the tabernacle which is called the Holiest of all; 4. Which had the golden censer, and the ark*

*of the covenant overlaid round about with gold,
wherein was the golden pot that had manna, and Aaron's
rod that budded, and the tables of the covenant; 5. And
over it the cherubims of glory shadowing the mercyseat; of
which we cannot now speak particularly. 6. Now when
these things were thus ordained, the priests went always
into the first tabernacle, accomplishing the service of God.
7. But into the second went the high priest alone once every
year, not without blood, which he offered for himself,
and for the errors of the people: 8. The Holy Ghost this
signifying, that the way into the holiest of all was not yet
made manifest, while as the first tabernacle was yet
standing: 9. Which was a figure for the time then present,
in which were offered both gifts and sacrifices, that could
not make him that did the service perfect, as pertaining to
the conscience; 10. Which stood only in meats and drinks,
and divers washings, and carnal ordinances, imposed on
them until the time of reformation.*

Redemption Through the Blood of Christ

*11. But Christ being come an high priest of good things to
come, by a greater and more perfect tabernacle, not made
with hands, that is to say, not of this building; 12. Neither
by the blood of goats and calves, but by his own blood he
entered in once into the holy place, having obtained
eternal redemption for us. 13. For if the blood of bulls and
of goats, and the ashes of an heifer sprinkling the unclean,
sanctifieth to the purifying of the flesh: 14. How much*

26

more shall the blood of Christ, who through the eternal Spirit offered himself without spot to God, purge your conscience from dead works to serve the living God? 15. And for this cause he is the mediator of the New Testament, that by means of death, for the redemption of the transgressions that were under the first testament, they which are called might receive the promise of eternal inheritance. 16. For where a testament is, there must also of necessity be the death of the testator. 17. For a testament is of force after men are dead: otherwise it is of no strength at all while the testator liveth. 18. Whereupon neither the first testament was dedicated without blood. 19. For when Moses had spoken every precept to all the people according to the law, he took the blood of calves and of goats, with water, and scarlet wool, and hyssop, and sprinkled both the book, and all the people, 20. Saying, this is the blood of the testament which God hath enjoined unto you. 21. Moreover, he sprinkled with blood both the tabernacle, and all the vessels of the ministry. 22. And almost all things are by the law purged with blood; and without shedding of blood is no remission. 23. It was therefore necessary that the patterns of things in the heavens should be purified with these; but the heavenly things themselves with better sacrifices than these. 24. For Christ is not entered into the holy places made with hands, which are the figures of the true; but into heaven itself, now to appear in the presence of God for us: 25. Nor yet that he should offer himself often, as the high priest entereth into the holy place every year with blood of others; 26. For then must he often have suffered since the foundation of the world: but now once in the end of the world hath he appeared to put away sin by the sacrifice of himself. 27. And as it is appointed unto men once to die, but after this the judgment: 28. So Christ was once offered to bear the sins of many; and unto them that look for him shall he appear the second time without sin unto salvation.

Hebrews 9:1-28: This chapter delves into the symbolism of the earthly tabernacle and the rituals performed by the Levitical priests, including the annual Day of Atonement sacrifices, as a foreshadowing of the ultimate sacrifice of Christ. The blood of animal sacrifices could only provide temporary purification, while the blood of Christ, as the perfect sacrifice, cleanses believers from sin once and for all. The author underscores the necessity of Christ's sacrificial death as the fulfillment of God's plan for redemption and the establishment of a new covenant reality, that brings eternal salvation, healing, deliverance, and reconciliation with God, to all who believe.
Praise the Lord! This has to be the premise by which we serve him and praise him all the days of our lives. He is the Lamb of God, slain before the foundation of this world. His love for us is unmeasurable and eternal.

Hebrews Chapter 10 says; *1. For the law having a shadow of good things to come, and not the very image of the things, can never with those sacrifices which they offered year by year continually make the comers*

thereunto perfect. 2. For then would they not have ceased to be offered? because that the worshippers once purged should have had no more conscience of sins. 3. But in those sacrifices there is a remembrance again made of sins every year. 4. For it is not possible that the blood of bulls and of goats should take away sins. 5. Wherefore when he cometh into the world, he saith, Sacrifice and offering thou wouldest not, but a body hast thou prepared me: 6. In burnt offerings and sacrifices for sin thou hast had no pleasure. 7. Then said I, Lo, I come (in the volume of the book it is written of me,) to do thy will, O God.
8. Above when he said, Sacrifice and offering and burnt offerings and offering for sin thou wouldest not, neither hadst pleasure therein; which are offered by the law;
9. Then said he, Lo, I come to do thy will, O God. He taketh away the first, that he may establish the second.
10. By the which will we are sanctified through the offering of the body of Jesus Christ once for all.
11. And every priest standeth daily ministering and offering oftentimes the same sacrifices, which can never take away sins:
12. But this man, after he had offered one sacrifice for sins forever, sat down on the right hand of God;
13. From henceforth expecting till his enemies be made his footstool.
14. For by one offering he hath perfected forever them that are sanctified.
15. Whereof the Holy Ghost also is a witness to us: for after that he had said before,

16. This is the covenant that I will make with them after those days, saith the Lord, I will put my laws into their hearts, and in their minds will I write them.
17. And their sins and iniquities will I remember no more.
18. Now where remission of these is, there is no more offering for sin.

The Full Assurance of Faith

19. Having therefore, brethren, boldness to enter into the holiest by the blood of Jesus, 20. By a new and living way, which he hath consecrated for us, through the veil, that is to say, his flesh; 21. And having an high priest over the house of God; 22. Let us draw near with a true heart in full assurance of faith, having our hearts sprinkled from an evil conscience, and our bodies washed with pure water. 23. Let us hold fast the profession of our faith without wavering; (for he is faithful that promised;) 24. And let us consider one another to provoke unto love and to good works: 25. Not forsaking the assembling of ourselves together, as the manner of some is; but exhorting one another: and so much the more, as ye see the day approaching. 26. For if we sin wilfully after that we have received the knowledge of the truth, there remaineth no more sacrifice for sins, 27. But a certain fearful looking for of judgment and fiery indignation, which shall devour the adversaries. 28. He that despised Moses' law died without mercy under two or three witnesses: 29. Of how much

30

sorer punishment, suppose ye, shall he be thought worthy, who hath trodden under foot the Son of God, and hath counted the blood of the covenant, wherewith he was sanctified, an unholy thing, and hath done despite unto the Spirit of grace? 30. For we know him that hath said, Vengeance belongeth unto me, I will recompense, saith the Lord. And again, The Lord shall judge his people. 31. It is a fearful thing to fall into the hands of the living God.

32. But call to remembrance the former days, in which, after ye were illuminated, ye endured a great fight of afflictions; 33. Partly, whilst ye were made a gazingstock both by reproaches and afflictions; and partly, whilst ye became companions of them that were so used. 34. For ye had compassion of me in my bonds, and took joyfully the spoiling of your goods, knowing in yourselves that ye have in heaven a better and an enduring substance. 35. Cast not away therefore your confidence, which hath great recompence of reward. 36. For ye have need of patience, that, after ye have done the will of God, ye might receive the promise. 37. For yet a little while, and he that shall come will come, and will not tarry. 38. Now the just shall live by faith: but if any man draw back, my soul shall have no pleasure in him. 39. But we are not of them who draw back unto perdition; but of them that believe to the saving of the soul.

Hebrews 10:1-39: The author further emphasizes the finality and sufficiency of Christ's sacrifice, contrasting it with the repetitive nature of the Old Covenant sacrifices. By offering himself as a perfect sacrifice, Christ has accomplished what the blood of bulls and goats could never achieve. Believers are called to draw near to God with full assurance of faith, knowing that their sins have been forgiven through the once-for-all sacrifice of Christ. The author encourages believers to hold fast to their confession of faith and to persevere in their walk with God, confident in the hope that Christ's sacrifice has secured for them. Believers are called to live this Life in the fulness of his goodness and in the riches of his Blessing because the priesthood has changed.

A life of faith

They speak to the core of our being, reminding us that faith is not just a fleeting emotion or a fleeting belief, but a substantial reality that shapes our existence.

32

Notes

Chapter 4

The Reality of "Now Faith Is" in the New Covenant Reality

In this chapter I want to take the time to explain the revelation God has given me about "Now Faith Is".

In the ancient words of the book of Hebrews, we find a profound declaration that resonates through the corridors of time, echoing the eternal truth about the nature of faith. *"Now faith is the substance of things hoped for, the evidence of things not seen."* (**Hebrews 11:1**)

These words, penned by an unknown author, capture the essence of what it means to live by faith.
Faith is, first and foremost, the substance of things hoped for. It is the confident assurance that what we hope for will come to pass, even though we may not see it with our physical eyes. It is the unwavering trust in the Covenant reality of God, the firm conviction that He who has promised has faithfully fulfilled through the completion of his sacrifice on the tree when he shed his blood for you and me.

Throughout the pages of the Bible, we see numerous examples of men and women who lived by faith, trusting in God's promises even when circumstances seemed bleak. Abraham, the father of faith, believed God's promise of a son in his old age, and it was credited to him as righteousness **(Genesis 15:6)**. Moses trusted in God's deliverance of the Israelites from slavery in Egypt, leading them through the wilderness to the promised land. **(Hebrews 11:24-29)**.

Faith is substance or matter. It exists all by itself. I remember when the Lord began to show me this revelation. I was preaching in a church in Peterborough Ontario, and I saw a guitar hanging on the wall of the church's platform when the spirit of God began to reveal to me that before that guitar was made, it was matter or substance.

It was wood, and it already existed, even if you did not see the finished product with your physical eyes. Faith always is, and it's what will cause God's creative power to flow in your life, but before we see the finished product in our lives, we must place wood, (meaning faith) in the hands of God and let him create.

Webster's dictionary defines "substance" as: something concrete, assurance, confidence. Something that exists by itself. That which is real, something real not imaginary, something solid, not empty.

Therefore:
1. Faith exists.
2. Faith is real.
3. Faith is solid.

We need to build our lives on something that exists and is real and is also solid. We need to build our lives on faith. And it is only substance to what we are hoping for.
Hope means a happy anticipation or expectation of something good.
So, let's start expecting with full anticipation of something only God can do in our lives, in Jesus' name.

I believe one of the problems is that the church's expectation level has depleted. We are more concerned about being entertained than moving in faith, and I believe one of the reasons is that we have not understood the new covenant reality.

I will always remember being in prayer and having the Lord speak to me. It was so clear and direct, He said, "Son, I want you to stop believing in a promise-based theology and start living in a new covenant reality." That was the moment things began to change in my life.

He said to me, "Faith will never be in the NOW if you live by a promise-based theology, because a promise is always something that is in your future and never in the now. A promise is something that is going to come to pass, and many of the things that God had promised in scripture have already come to pass. They have already happened. They are not going to happen. They are not going to become real. They have already become real. This is why it is important that we understand that we are not living under the promise of salvation or healing or even freedom in our lives. We are living in the covenant of salvation, healing and freedom! Now, it's not going to come to pass, it has already come to pass. Through the precious Blood of Christ, we no longer have a promise, we now have a covenant that must become a reality."

Let me give you an example of this. In 1993, around Christmas time, I decided I was going to make a promise to my girlfriend Teena Cooper. I was in love with her, and I had decided I wanted to live the rest of my life with this beautiful woman that God brought into my life. I decided I was going to buy a dozen roses and a ring to put on her finger, and ask her if she would marry me, and give me the honor to be her husband. So, I got everything I needed to get, and in her home at 83 Candlewood Drive, Moncton, NB I got down on one knee and asked her to be my wife. It was the best day of my life when she said, "Yes"!

Now, that was a promise. In July of 1994 I made good on my word. I took the promise to the next level. I met her at the church and watched the most beautiful woman I had ever seen walk down the aisle of the church. She stood beside me, and we made vows to each other, before Pastor Bill and God, and became husband and wife.

The next morning, she did not have to wonder if I was her husband, she knew I was her husband, and she was my wife. In this moment, as I am writing this book, it has been 30 years since I made that covenant with her, and we have lived in the reality of this covenant. She never wonders if she can live in our house, eat our food that is in the fridge, and spend my money (oh, sorry, our money!). She knows what's mine is hers and what's hers is hers, not because she has a promise, but because we have a covenant. The faith we have in each other became a "now" moment from the moment we made a covenant.

The same with God! What was His is now ours, because faith is never in your future and it is no longer based on a promise, but on an everlasting covenant with God. From the moment Christ spilled his blood on the old cross, we went from having a promise to having the privilege of living a "NOW FAITH, COVENANT REALITY LIFE".

The evidence of things not seen is the second aspect of faith highlighted in **Hebrews 11:1**. It is the conviction that transcends the limitations of our senses, enabling us to perceive the invisible realities of the spiritual realm. It is through faith that we understand that the universe was created by the Word of God, so that what is seen was not made from things that are visible (**Hebrews 11:3**).

As believers, we are called to walk by faith and not by sight (**2 Corinthians 5:7**). This means living each day with a deep trust in God's ability to perform his word in our lives even when we cannot see the outcome of our circumstances. It means holding fast to His new covenant reality in our lives, knowing that He is faithful to fulfill them in our lives.

In a world that often values tangible evidence and empirical proof, faith stands as a counter-cultural declaration of the reality of the covenant. It is the anchor for our souls, the assurance of things hoped for, the evidence of things not seen. May we, like the heroes of faith before us, walk in the reality of faith, trusting in the God who is able to do immeasurably more than all we ask or imagine (**Ephesians 3:20**).

The Essence of Living by Faith

In the tapestry of human existence, woven with the threads of time and eternity, faith stands as a radiant jewel, illuminating the path of those who dare to believe beyond what the eyes can see. **Hebrews 11:1** beckons us to contemplate the profound nature of faith, offering us a glimpse into the spiritual truth of living in a new covenant reality right now. "Now faith is the substance of things hoped for, the evidence of things not seen."

Faith is also evidence.

- Evidence- Proof of substance, well furnished, obvious to the eyes.

- Faith is the foundation upon which our spiritual lives are built, the assurance that what we hope for will come to pass, even though we cannot see it with our physical eyes yet.

These words, written by the unknown author of the book of Hebrews, resonate through the ages, inviting us to delve deeper into the mysteries of faith and its transformative power in the lives of believers.

Faith, the substance of things hoped for, is not a mere wishful thinking or a fleeting sentiment but a steadfast confidence in the covenant of God. It is the anchor of our souls, grounding us in the hope that transcends the limitations of the present moment. Just as Abraham believed in the promise of a son in his old age and Moses trusted in God's deliverance of the Israelites, we are called to embrace the substance of our hopes with unwavering trust in the faithfulness of our Creator.

Throughout the tapestry of Scripture, we encounter a gallery of faith-filled individuals who walked in the reality of their beliefs. By faith, Noah built an ark to save his family from the flood. By faith, Rahab welcomed the spies and was spared. By faith, David faced Goliath with a sling and a stone. These heroes of faith exemplify the transformative power of belief in God's covenant, demonstrating that faith is not passive acceptance but active participation in God's redemptive plan.

The evidence of things not seen is the other facet of faith that **Hebrews 11:1** illuminates. It is the spiritual lens through which we perceive the invisible realities of the kingdom of God, recognizing that the visible world is sustained by the unseen hand of the Creator. By faith, we understand that the universe was created by the Word of God, that what is seen was not made out of things that are visible. This profound insight invites us to transcend the limitations of empirical evidence and embrace the deeper truths that lie beyond the veil of the material world.

Living by faith requires a radical shift in perspective, a willingness to surrender our need for control and certainty and trust in God's Word to guide our steps. It means walking in obedience to God's Word, even when the path ahead seems uncertain, and clinging to His covenant with unwavering faith. It is a journey of transformation, for our souls that leads us from darkness to light, from doubt to certainty, from fear to courage.
As we embark on this journey of faith, may we draw strength from the cloud of witnesses who have gone before us, the men and women of old who lived by faith and saw

the fulfillment of God's promises in their lives. May their stories inspire us to embrace the reality of faith in the new covenant reality, to walk in the substance of things hoped for and the evidence of things not seen, knowing that our faith is the key that unlocks the door to the abundant life that God has prepared for those who love Him.

Notes

Chapter 5

The Guarantee of the New Covenant Reality

Jesus as the Guarantee of the New Covenant
The concept of Jesus serving as the guarantee of the New Covenant is a fundamental aspect of Christian belief. This idea is deeply rooted in the Bible and is articulated in various passages that emphasize Jesus' role as the mediator. He is the go-between with God and humanity. We will explore the significance of Jesus as the guarantee of the New Covenant, established through the sacrifice of Jesus Christ. This stands as the cornerstone of Christian faith, salvation, healing and freedom. Jesus, as the guarantor of this new covenant reality is assuring us of the fulfillment of God's Word in our lives.
John 14:12-14, John 15:16, John 16:23-24, Philippians 2:1-11, and **Acts 4:8-13**.

Hebrews 7:22-25 (The Message Bible)
22. This makes Jesus the guarantee of a far better way between us and God—one that really works!

A new covenant. 23. Earlier there were a lot of priests, for they died and had to be replaced. 24. But Jesus' priesthood is permanent. He's there from now to eternity

25. to save everyone who comes to God through him, always on the job to speak up for them.

Jesus is High Priest of the New Covenant in **Hebrews 7:22-25**, where Jesus is portrayed as the guarantor of a better covenant. The passage highlights Jesus' role as the eternal High Priest who intercedes on behalf of all believers before God.

Unlike the Levitical priests who offered sacrifices repeatedly, Jesus offered himself once and for all as the perfect sacrifice for sin and redemption. Through his sacrificial death and resurrection, Jesus secures eternal redemption for those who believe in him. He stands as the mediator between God and humanity, ensuring access to God's grace and forgiveness under the New Covenant.

So, having said all that, I know that in the last decade there has been argument about preaching Grace versus the Law. I just want to say that we should preach the New Covenant Reality of God. His covenant is not coming; it has come. In Jesus, the blood has been spilled, the sacrifice has been made, and the Guarantor is alive and well, and able to perform his Word in our lives, in Jesus' name.

By offering himself as a perfect sacrifice for sin, Jesus establishes a new covenant reality in our lives that is based on grace, truth and forgiveness. Through his sacrificial death and resurrection, Jesus secures eternal salvation, healing, deliverance and prosperity for those who believe in him, serving as the ultimate guarantee of the New Covenant reality in our lives.

The new covenant reality name, and the guarantee of the power of his covenant is in the mighty Name of Jesus.

John 14:12-14

12. Verily, verily, I say unto you, He that believeth on me, the works that I do shall he do also; and greater works than these shall he do, because I go unto my Father. 13. And whatsoever ye shall ask in my name, that will I do, that the Father may be glorified in the Son. 14. If ye shall ask any thing in my name, I will do it.

In **John 14:12-14** Jesus speaks about the authority granted to all believers through him. He assures his disciples and his followers that they will perform even greater works than he did, emphasizing the power of faith and the importance of prayer. By invoking his name, believers can access the divine authority and the new covenant reality of God. This demonstrates Jesus' role as the guarantor of blessings and of the covenant by answering prayers within the framework of the New Covenant Name: Jesus.

The name *Jesus* assures his disciples of the authority and power granted to believers through him. His Covenant reality to those who believe in him will do even greater works than he did. That is what God the Father wants. He wants to see us do the greater works by using the name that is above every other name, the name of Jesus. Whatever we ask in his name will be granted to us. The significance of faith, prayer, and reliance on Jesus as the guarantor of the New Covenant Reality is seeing our prayers being answered within the context of the New Covenant Reality.

Within the New Covenant, Jesus declares that his disciples did not choose him but rather he chose them and appointed them to bear fruit that will last. This passage emphasizes Jesus' sovereign authority in selecting and empowering individuals for his purposes, highlighting his role as the guarantor of divine calling and empowerment within the framework of the New Covenant.

Knowing that we are never alone when we step out in his name, we never have to feel the responsibility of having to perform the miracle. We must only step out in faith knowing we do the "asking" and he does the "doing". The responsibility is on him to perform what Faith has asked in Jesus' name. Jesus is the one who chooses and appoints his disciples for a specific purpose. Jesus declares that his followers did not choose him but that he chose them, and I love him because he first loved me.

John 16:23 *in that day ye shall ask me nothing. Verily, verily, I say unto you, Whatsoever ye shall ask the Father in my name, he will give it you.* **John 16:24** *Hitherto have ye asked nothing in my name: ask, and ye shall receive, that your joy may be full.*

John 16:23-24, Jesus emphasizes the direct access believers have to God through Him. He instructs his followers to ask the Father in His name, promising that their prayers will be answered. Jesus' role as the mediator between humanity and God, provides believers with assurance that their petitions will be granted through their connection to Him as the guarantor of the New Covenant Reality.

In conclusion, Jesus illustrates that He is the guarantor of the New Covenant. Through his sacrificial death, resurrection, and ongoing intercession, Jesus serves as the mediator, high priest, and source of authority for believers, ensuring the fulfillment of God's Covenant and the establishment of a new relationship between humanity and God. Embracing Jesus as the guarantee of the New Covenant is essential for experiencing the fullness of God in our lives.

As we see in **Philippians chapter 2, verses 1-11**; *1. If there be therefore any consolation in Christ, if any comfort of love, if any fellowship of the Spirit, if any bowels and mercies, 2. Fulfil ye my joy, that ye be likeminded, having the same love, being of one accord, of*

48

one mind. 3. Let nothing be done through strife or vainglory; but in lowliness of mind let each esteem other better than themselves. 4. Look not every man on his own things, but every man also on the things of others. 5. Let this mind be in you, which was also in Christ Jesus: 6. Who, being in the form of God, thought it not robbery to be equal with God: 7. But made himself of no reputation, and took upon him the form of a servant, and was made in the likeness of men: 8. And being found in fashion as a man, he humbled himself, and became obedient unto death, even the death of the cross. 9. Wherefore God also hath highly exalted him, and given him a name which is above every name:10. That at the name of Jesus every knee should bow, of things in heaven, and things in earth, and things under the earth;11. And that every tongue should confess that Jesus Christ is Lord, to the glory of God the Father.

Philippians 2:1-11 portrays the humility and exaltation of Jesus Christ. Despite being in the form of God, Jesus emptied himself, taking on the form of a servant and humbling himself to the point of death on a cross. As a result of his obedience, God exalted him to the highest place and bestowed on him the name above every name. This passage highlights Jesus' obedience and sacrificial love, making Him the guarantor of salvation and the embodiment of the New Covenant Reality.

Chapter 6

Walking in New Covenant Reality - Considering Not the Natural

When we walk in the reality of the New Covenant, we are called to live a life that transcends the natural limitations and constraints of this world. The New Covenant, established through the blood of Jesus Christ, offers us a higher way of living, rooted in faith and empowered by the Holy Spirit. In this chapter, we will explore the importance of considering not the natural when walking in the New Covenant, drawing inspiration from this new reality.

Romans 4:16-21

16Therefore it is of faith that it might be according to grace, so that the promise might be sure to all the seed, not only to those who are of the law, but also to those who are of the faith of Abraham, who is the father of us all 17(as it is written, "I have made you a father of many nations") in the presence of Him whom he believed—

God, who gives life to the dead and calls those things which do not exist as though they did; ¹⁸who, contrary to hope, in hope believed, so that he became the father of many nations according to what was spoken, "So shall your descendants be." ¹⁹And not being weak in faith he did not consider his own body, already dead (since he was about a hundred years old), and the deadness of Sarah's womb. ²⁰He did not waver at the promise of God through unbelief, but was strengthened in faith, giving glory to God, ²¹and being fully convinced that what He had promised He was able to perform.

In **Romans 4:16-21**, the apostle Paul writes about the faith of Abraham, the father of all who believe, and how he was justified by faith rather than by works of the law. Paul emphasizes that the promise comes by faith so that it may be according to grace, guaranteeing its fulfillment to all Abraham's descendants, not only to those who are of the law but also to those who have the faith of Abraham.

Abraham's faith serves as a powerful example of what it means to walk in the New Covenant reality. In verse 17, Paul highlights how Abraham believed in God, who gives life to the dead and calls into existence things that do not exist. This speaks to the essence of faith in the New Covenant – believing in the supernatural power of God to bring about His promises, even when circumstances seem impossible in the natural realm.

We, as new covenant reality believers must do as Abraham did. He called into existence the things that did not exist. He spoke the word of God, contrary to the natural situation and circumstance that was present in his life. My Grandmother Cormier had a saying that she would say to me, "If you have nothing good to say, then say nothing at all." Even though that sounds good, I believe that if we have nothing good to say, we should speak the Word of God. Saying nothing changes nothing, whereas speaking the word of God in faith can change everything.

As believers in the New Covenant, we are called to follow in the footsteps of Abraham, considering not the natural limitations or obstacles that we may face. Instead, we are to fix our eyes on the Word of God, knowing that He is faithful to fulfill what He has spoken. In verse 18, Paul describes how Abraham, against all hope, believed in hope, and so became the father of many nations, just as God had promised him.

Often in our lives, we will fight against situations and circumstances that will try to bring a state of hopelessness, but against all odds, we must believe the Word of God and stand on his New Covenant in our lives.

Walking in the New Covenant reality requires a shift in perspective – from focusing on what is seen in the natural, to trusting in the unseen realities of God's kingdom. This kind of faith enables us to overcome doubt, fear, and discouragement, as we anchor our souls in the unchanging character of God. As Paul concludes in verse 21, Abraham was fully convinced that God was able to do what He had promised, and this unwavering faith was credited to him as righteousness.

In our journey of faith in the New Covenant, let us emulate the faith of Abraham, considering not the natural circumstances, but holding fast to the promises of God. As we walk in this supernatural reality, we will experience the power and provision of God in ways that transcend human understanding, bringing glory to His name and fulfillment to His purpose in our lives.

Stand against natural circumstances and speak the Word.

1. In the presence of sickness, speak life.
2. In the presence of fear, speak peace.
3. In the presence of bondage and addiction, speak freedom.
4. In the presence of poverty and lack, speak abundance and prosperity.
5. In the presence of darkness and despair, speak light and strength.

We must not let our situation predict our outcome. In the New Covenant Reality Jesus is the final authority in our lives.

In the New Covenant Reality, I have been declared Righteous.

In the New Covenant Reality, one of the most profound truths that believers can rejoice in is the declaration of righteousness that comes through faith in Jesus Christ. The apostle Paul's letter to the Romans, specifically **Romans 3:21-25**, illuminates this foundational aspect of the New Covenant and the transformative power it holds for those who believe.

Romans 3:21-25 (NIV) reads:

"But now apart from the law the righteousness of God has been made known, to which the Law and the Prophets testify. This righteousness is given through faith in Jesus Christ to all who believe. There is no difference between Jew and Gentile, for all have sinned and fall short of the glory of God, and all are justified freely by his grace through the redemption that came by Christ Jesus."

In these verses, Paul unveils a central theme of the New Covenant: the righteousness of God that is revealed apart from the law. This righteousness is not earned through adherence to religious rituals or moral codes but is bestowed as a gift through faith in Jesus Christ. It is a righteousness that transcends human merit and is available to all who believe, regardless of their background or past failures.

As participants in the New Covenant Reality, we are invited to embrace this profound truth of being declared righteous before God. The reality of our sin and shortcomings is acknowledged, as Paul emphasizes that all have sinned and fall short of God's glory. However, the beauty of the New Covenant shines forth in the next statement – that we are justified freely by God's grace through the redemption found in Christ Jesus.

Through the sacrificial death and resurrection of Jesus Christ, a way has been made for us to be reconciled to God and declared righteous in His sight. Our sins are forgiven, our guilt is removed, and we are clothed in the righteousness of Christ Himself. This is not a righteousness that we achieve through our own efforts but a righteousness that is imputed to us by faith in the finished work of Jesus on the cross.

In the New Covenant Reality, our identity is no longer defined by our past mistakes or shortcomings. Instead, we are seen through the lens of God's grace and mercy, as those who have been justified and made righteous through faith in Christ. This truth empowers us to walk in freedom, confidence, and intimacy with God, knowing that we stand before Him covered in the righteousness of His Son.

As we embrace the reality of being declared righteous in the New Covenant, may we live out our lives in gratitude, worship, and obedience, reflecting the love and grace of our Heavenly Father to a world in need of His redeeming power.

In the New Covenant Reality believers are transformed into temples of the Holy Spirit.

In the New Covenant Reality, believers are not only declared righteous through faith in Jesus Christ but are also transformed into temples of the Holy Spirit, where God's presence dwells and His glory shines forth. The apostle Paul, in his second letter to the Corinthians, highlights this profound truth in **2 Corinthians 6:16-18**, revealing the intimate relationship between believers and the living God.

2 Corinthians 6:16-18 (NIV) states:

"What agreement is there between the temple of God and idols? For we are the temple of the living God. As God has said: 'I will live with them and walk among them, and I will be their God, and they will be my people.' Therefore, 'Come out from them and be separate, says the Lord. Touch no unclean thing, and I will receive you.' And 'I will be a Father to you, and you will be my sons and daughters,' says the Lord Almighty."

In these verses, Paul draws a parallel between the temple of God in the Old Testament and the spiritual reality of believers in the New Covenant. Just as the temple in

Jerusalem was a sacred place where God's presence dwelt among His people, so too are believers now the dwelling place of the living God through the indwelling of the Holy Spirit. As temples of the Holy Spirit, we are set apart for God's purposes and empowered to live holy and righteous lives. The presence of God within us not only sanctifies us but also guides, comforts, and empowers us to fulfill the calling and destiny that He has ordained for our lives. We are no longer mere mortals but vessels through which the glory of God can manifest in the world.

The privilege of being the temple of the Holy Spirit comes with a call to purity and separation from the ways of the world. We are exhorted to come out from the influence of darkness, to touch no unclean thing, and to live in a manner that reflects the holiness of our God. This separation is not one of isolation but of consecration, as we are called to be a light in the midst of a dark and broken world.

Furthermore, as temples of the Holy Spirit, we are embraced as beloved children of God, adopted into His family and granted the privilege of intimate fellowship with Him. We are not only servants or subjects but sons and daughters of the Highest, heirs of His kingdom and recipients of His abundant love and provision.

In the New Covenant Reality, may we embrace the truth that we are the temple of the Holy Spirit, consecrated for God's glory and empowered by His presence within us. Let us walk in the awareness of His indwelling Spirit, living as vessels of His grace, love, and power in a world that desperately needs the light of Christ to shine through us.

Declared Healed in the New Covenant Reality

In the New Covenant Reality, believers are not only declared righteous and temples of the Holy Spirit but are also declared healed by the redemptive work of Jesus Christ. The Scriptures in Isaiah 53:5 and 1 Peter 2:24 beautifully illustrate this profound truth, revealing the healing power that is made available to all who put their trust in the finished work of the cross of Christ.

Isaiah 53:5 (NIV) prophesies about the suffering and atoning work of the Messiah, declaring:

"But he was pierced for our transgressions, he was crushed for our iniquities; the punishment that brought us peace was on him, and by his wounds we are healed."

These words penned centuries before Christ's earthly ministry, foreshadow the sacrificial death of Jesus on the cross and the healing that would be made available to all who believe in Him. The physical, emotional, and spiritual healing that humanity desperately needs is found in the wounds borne by the suffering Servant, who took upon

Himself our sins and infirmities to bring us wholeness and restoration.

In **1 Peter 2:24** (NIV), the apostle Peter reaffirms this truth in the context of Christ's redemptive work, stating:

"He himself bore our sins in his body on the cross, so that we might die to sins and live for righteousness; by his wounds you have been healed."

Peter emphasizes that through the atoning sacrifice of Jesus, not only are our sins forgiven and our spirits made alive in righteousness, but our bodies and minds are also touched by the healing power of His wounds. The healing that Christ provides is comprehensive, addressing every aspect of our being and restoring us to the wholeness and vitality that God intended for His creation.

In the New Covenant Reality, the declaration of healing is not merely a promise for the future but a present reality that we can lay hold of by faith. The stripes that Jesus bore on His back are not only symbols of our forgiveness but also symbols of our healing, pointing to the restoration and renewal that He offers to all who come to Him in faith.

As participants in the New Covenant, may we embrace the truth that we are declared healed by the stripes of Jesus Christ. Let us walk in the reality of this healing, trusting in the power of His sacrifice to bring wholeness, restoration, and health to every area of our lives. May we live as testimonies of His healing grace, proclaiming to the world that in Christ, true and lasting healing is found.

Embracing Freedom in the New Covenant Reality

In the New Covenant Reality, believers are called to walk in the freedom that Christ has purchased for them through His sacrificial death and resurrection. The Scriptures in Galatians, Ephesians, and Romans beautifully illustrate the transformative power of this freedom and the invitation to live in accordance with the truth and grace of the Gospel.

In **Galatians 4:24-31** (NIV), the apostle Paul uses the allegory of Hagar and Sarah to illustrate the distinction between living under the law and living in freedom through faith in Christ. Paul emphasizes that believers are children of promise, born not into slavery but into freedom, symbolized by the Jerusalem above, which is free.
We are not children with a promise, we are the children of promise, and in this we can walk in freedom in our lives.

Galatians 5:1 (NIV) echoes this theme of freedom, declaring: *"It is for freedom that Christ has set us free. Stand firm, then, and do not let yourselves be burdened again by a yoke of slavery."* Through the redemptive work of Christ, believers are liberated from the bondage of sin, legalism, and fear, and are empowered to walk in the liberty of the Spirit, guided by love and grace.

 Ephesians 4:17-18 (NIV) highlights the contrast between the old way of life, characterized by futility and darkness, and the new way of life in Christ: *"So I tell you this, and insist on it in the Lord, that you must no longer live as the Gentiles do, in the futility of their thinking. They are darkened in their understanding and separated from the life of God because of the ignorance that is in them due to the hardening of their hearts."*

In **Ephesians 4:23-24a** (NIV), believers are encouraged to be renewed in the spirit of their minds and to put on the new self, created to be like God in true righteousness and holiness. This transformation of the mind and heart is essential for walking in the freedom and fullness of life that Christ offers to His followers.

Romans 12:2 (NIV) further emphasizes the renewal of the mind as a key aspect of experiencing true freedom in Christ: *"Do not conform to the pattern of this world but be transformed by the renewing of your mind. Then you will be able to test and approve what God's will is—his good, pleasing and perfect will."*

In the New Covenant Reality, believers are called to embrace the freedom that Christ has secured for them, walking in the truth, grace, and power of the Gospel. This freedom is not merely an absence of constraints but a liberation to live in alignment with God's will, reflecting His love, righteousness, and glory to the world. As we renew our minds, surrender our hearts, and walk in the Spirit, we will experience the abundant life and liberty that Christ offers to all who believe in Him.

Notes

Chapter 7

The Man Who Did Not Know He Had a Covenant

The Covenant of Mephibosheth
In the land of Israel, during the time of King David's reign, there lived a man named Mephibosheth. Little did he know that a covenant made long ago would change his life forever.

Mephibosheth was the son of Jonathan, the beloved friend of King David. Unfortunately, Mephibosheth had a tragic past. When he was just a young child, news of his father's and grandfather's deaths reached the household. In the chaos and confusion that followed, a nursemaid picked up Mephibosheth to flee the palace. In her haste, she stumbled and dropped the young boy, leaving him crippled in both feet.

In **2Samuel Chapter 4**, beginning at verse 1, we read:
1. And when Saul's son heard that Abner was dead in Hebron, his hands were feeble, and all the Israelites were troubled.

2. And Saul's son had two men that were captains of bands: the name of the one was Baanah, and the name of the other Rechab, the sons of Rimmon a Beerothite, of the children of Benjamin: (for Beeroth also was reckoned to Benjamin:
3. And the Beerothites fled to Gittaim and were sojourners there until this day.)
4. And Jonathan, Saul's son, had a son that was lame of his feet. He was five years old when the tidings came of Saul and Jonathan out of Jezreel, and his nurse took him up, and fled: and it came to pass, as she made haste to flee, that he fell, and became lame. And his name was Mephibosheth.

Mephibosheth was given a name that was encompassed by his life experience, the meaning of his name is translated as follows;
Mephib- to blow away, to break into pieces, to shatter.
Bosheth- Shameful thing

I can't imagine having an experience in life where it's not even your fault, because someone dropped you and you are given the name a "Broken Shameful Thing". That name is given to you because of your condition.

It reminds me of when I was a young boy growing up in a small community and having people calling me "the epileptic" or "retarded" because of a physical condition I had called epilepsy. I had teachers in school who would punish me for falling asleep in class and would call me stupid and treated me very poorly. They would send me to the principal, and I would get the strap on the hand, all because I had epilepsy and had to take medication that would cause me to fall asleep in class. It made it hard for me to focus in class.

Thanks be unto God my condition was not my conclusion, and at the age of twelve my Uncle Arthur came home from London Ontario, and on his way up in the car the spirit of God spoke to him and said, "You're going to lay your hand on Brian and pray, and he will never have another epileptic seizure in his life." So, May 22, 1985, was the last day I took any medication or ever again had an epileptic seizure. Next year I will celebrate 40 years of being healed and saved! To God be the glory! He truly does turn everything the enemy means for bad into good.
So, let's continue with what happened with Mephibosheth.

Years passed, and Mephibosheth lived in the land of Lo-debar, a place of obscurity and insignificance. Unbeknownst to him, discussions were taking place in the royal court of King David that would change the course of his life.

The word Lo-debar is translated as;
Lo- meaning no, not, nothing, without, nay, never, out of.
Debar- meaning, pasture, hope, future, without word, speaking, manner.

Again, in 2Samuel we read in chapter 9;

1. One day David asked, "Is there anyone left of Saul's family? If so, I'd like to show him some kindness in honor of Jonathan."

2. It happened that a servant from Saul's household named Ziba was there. They called him into David's presence. The king asked him, "Are you Ziba?" "Yes sir," he replied.

3. The king asked, "Is there anyone left from the family of Saul to whom I can show some godly kindness?" Ziba told the king, "Yes, there is Jonathan's son, lame in both feet."

4. "Where is he?" "He's living at the home of Makir son of Ammiel in Lo Debar."

We could say that Mephibosheth was found in a place of no hope, no word, and no future, or a place of never having hope or a future or a word. That will always be the plan of the enemy in our lives to take us and leave us in a place of despair.

So, in the city of Hebron, where King David resided, there were murmurs of a covenant made between David and Jonathan. This covenant, forged in the midst of adversity and war, bound the two friends and their descendants together in a bond of loyalty and protection.

One day, messengers were sent out to search for any surviving members of Jonathan's family. Their quest led them to Lo-debar, where they discovered Mephibosheth living in a humble abode. The news of the king's summons filled Mephibosheth with fear and trepidation. He could not imagine what the king wanted from a crippled man living in obscurity.

Continuing in chapter 9 of 2Samuel;
5. King David didn't lose a minute. He sent and got him from the home of Makir son of Ammiel in Lo Debar.

6. When Mephibosheth son of Jonathan (who was the son of Saul), came before David, he bowed deeply, abasing himself, honoring David. David spoke his name: "Mephibosheth." "Yes sir?"
7. "Don't be frightened," said David. "I'd like to do something special for you in memory of your father Jonathan. To begin with, I'm returning to you all the properties of your grandfather Saul. Furthermore, from now on you'll take all your meals at my table."
8. Shuffling and stammering, not looking him in the eye, Mephibosheth said, "Who am I that you pay attention to a stray dog like me?"
9. David then called in Ziba, Saul's right-hand man, and told him, "Everything that belonged to Saul and his family, I've handed over to your master's grandson.
10. You and your sons and your servants will work his land and bring in the produce, provisions for your master's grandson. Mephibosheth himself, your master's grandson, from now on will take all his meals at my table." Ziba had fifteen sons and twenty servants.

68

*11. "All that my master the king has ordered his servant,"
answered Ziba, "your servant will surely do." And
Mephibosheth ate at David's table, just like one of the royal
family.
12. Mephibosheth also had a small son named Mica. All
who were part of Ziba's household were now the servants
of Mephibosheth.
13. Mephibosheth lived in Jerusalem, taking all his meals
at the king's table. He was lame in both feet.
As Mephibosheth was brought before King David, he fell
to the ground in fear and reverence. But to his
astonishment, the king spoke words of kindness and grace.
"Do not be afraid, for I will show you kindness for the sake
of your father Jonathan. I will restore to you all the land of
your grandfather Saul, and you shall eat at my table
always."*

When we know we have a covenant, it restores, in Jesus'
name, all that the devil has stolen from us. Everything was
restored to Mephibosheth because King David honored his
covenant with Jonathan, and he was no longer in the place
of "No Future". He was brought to his rightful place because
he was heir to the covenant.

He was overwhelmed by the king's generosity.
Mephibosheth could hardly believe his ears. He who
thought himself an outcast and unworthy was now invited
to dine at the king's table as one of his own sons. The

covenant made between David and Jonathan had found its fulfillment in the life of Mephibosheth.

From that day on, Mephibosheth's life was forever changed. He dwelt in the king's palace, feasting at the royal table and enjoying the favor and protection of the king. The man who did not know he had a covenant now lived in the fullness of its blessings, a living testimony to the grace and faithfulness of King David. And so, the story of Mephibosheth serves as a reminder that even in our brokenness and obscurity, God's covenant of grace and redemption is always at work, ready to transform our lives and bring us into the fullness of His blessings.

We need to conclude that if we are children of God, we are people with a covenant and we must learn to walk this Christian life with a new covenant reality. We must not be like Mephibosheth living in despair, but we must live our lives at the king's table knowing provision has already been made for us to have access and provision from our heavenly father. This is all because of the sacrifices of his only begotten son, Jesus Christ, who paid the ultimate price to provide a New Covenant Reality.

Notes

Chapter 8

Praying with a New Covenant Reality Perspective

When we understand the reality of the New Covenant, we can have a greater confidence and faith in our prayer life.

In exploring the concept of praying within the framework of a New Covenant reality, we turn to **Hebrews 7:11-17**, which discusses the superiority of Christ's priesthood compared to the Levitical priesthood. This passage helps us understand how our prayer life is shaped by the New Covenant established through Jesus Christ.

Hebrews 7:11-17 (NKJV)
11 Therefore, if perfection were through the Levitical priesthood (for under it the people received the law), what further need was there that another priest should rise according to the order of Melchizedek, and not be called according to the order of Aaron?
12 For the priesthood being changed, of necessity there is also a change of the law.

13 For He of whom these things are spoken belongs to another tribe, from which no man has officiated at the altar.
14 For it is evident that our Lord arose from Judah, of which tribe Moses spoke nothing concerning priesthood.
15 And it is yet far more evident if, in the likeness of Melchizedek, there arises another priest
16 who has come, not according to the law of a fleshly commandment, but according to the power of an endless life.
17 For He testifies: "You are a priest forever according to the order of Melchizedek."

Hebrews 7:11-17
11. The Need for a New Priesthood. The passage begins by establishing that the Levitical priesthood was insufficient for achieving perfection. This underscores the necessity for a new kind of priest—a priest "according to the order of Melchizedek." In prayer, this means we approach God not through human intermediaries but through the eternal priesthood of Christ.

A "Change of Law" in verse 12 states that with the change of the priesthood, there is a change in the law. This indicates that our approach to God is no longer based on the Old Covenant laws but through the grace and truth provided by Christ. Our prayers are thus grounded in grace, not legalism. Christ's Uniqueness in Verses 13-14 emphasize that Jesus, from the tribe of Judah, serves as our high priest. This is significant because it shows that He fulfills roles that were previously thought to be exclusive to the Levites, expanding the understanding of who can communicate with God.

An "Eternal Priesthood" in verses 15-17 highlight that Jesus' priesthood is eternal, based on the "power of an endless life." This reassures believers that our prayers are continually interceded for by Christ, who is always present and active.

Praying with Assurance
With this understanding, prayer from a New Covenant perspective is one of confidence and boldness.
Hebrews 4:16 encourages us to approach the throne of grace with confidence, knowing that we can receive mercy and grace in our time of need, thanks to Christ's eternal priesthood.

The Message Translation of **Hebrews 7:11-17**
11 If the old system of priestly rules could have worked out a perfect plan for the people, they would have never needed a new plan.
12 But since that old plan wasn't able to get the job done, a complete overhaul was in order.
13 Jesus, the high priest, was chosen not from the tribe of Levi, but from the tribe of Judah.
14 And that's not a minor detail; it's a key to the new way of doing things.

*15 This new priest, who is like Melchizedek, is a different
kind of priest.
16 He's not in it for the rules and regulations but for the
sheer power of an indestructible life. 17 That's what makes
Him a priest forever, in the order of Melchizedek.*

A Complete Overhaul

The Message translation emphasizes the need for a
complete overhaul of the old system. This conveys the
radical shift in how we relate to God. Our prayers are not
bound by outdated rituals but are infused with the dynamic
life of Christ.

A Different Kind of Priest

The description of Jesus as a different kind of priest
highlights His unique role and the freedom we have in
approaching God. Our prayers are direct communications
with the Father, empowered by the Holy Spirit.

Indestructible Life

The focus on "the sheer power of an indestructible life"
reassures us that our prayers are sustained by the very life
of Christ, eliminating any fear of rejection or inadequacy.

Praying from a New Covenant reality perspective involves
recognizing the transformative work of Christ as our high
priest. It allows us to pray with confidence and assurance,
knowing that we are heard and interceded for by an eternal
priest who understands our struggles. This perspective

shifts our prayer life from obligation to a vibrant relationship with God, characterized by grace, power, and intimacy. Through this lens, every prayer becomes a declaration of our faith in the finished work of Christ.

Jesus my High Priest is from a new tribe. He came from the tribe of Judah and **"Judah"** means Praise and Celebration as well as "to confess", and "thanksgiving". That is why the new covenant reality perspective to prayer leads us to praise and worship God for what we prayed for.

New Covenant Reality Perspective to Prayer:

In John 14:12-14, Jesus speaks to His disciples about the nature of their relationship with Him and the power of prayer in the context of the New Covenant. This passage offers profound insights into how believers can approach prayer, underlining the authority and access we have through Christ.

John 14:12-14 (NKJV)
12 "Most assuredly, I say to you, he who believes in Me, the works that I do he will do also; and greater works than these he will do, because I go to My Father.
13 And whatever you ask in My name, that I will do, that the Father may be glorified in the Son.
14 If you ask anything in My name, I will do it."

I believe that Jesus, in verse 12, emphasizes that belief in Him is foundational. This belief is not passive; it's an active trust that empowers believers to participate in His works. The phrase "greater works" suggests that through the empowerment of the Holy Spirit, believers will accomplish significant acts that reflect Christ's mission.

We are using the authority of His Name in verse 13, asking in Jesus' name. This is not a mere formula but an invitation to align one's requests with the character and will of Christ. When believers pray in His name, they invoke His authority, ensuring that the requests are consistent with His purpose and mission for our lives to glorify the Father The purpose of answered prayer, as stated in verse 13, is to glorify the Father through the Son. This highlights that prayer is not just about personal desires but is ultimately a means of honoring God. The New Covenant perspective shifts the focus of prayer from individual needs, to seeing the glory of God manifest in our lives.

In verse 14 we are assured that our prayers will be answered. This is a powerful example of the provision of a powerful promise: "If you ask anything in My name, I will do it." This assurance stems from the believer's relationship with Christ and the transformative power of the New Covenant, which allows for direct communication with God.

The Message Bible Translation of John 14:12-14

12 "The person who trusts me will not only do what I'm doing but even greater things because I, on my way to the Father, am giving you the same work to do.
13 You can count on me to do whatever you ask in my name. That's how the Father will be seen for who he is in the Son. 14 I mean it: Whatever you request along the lines of who I am and what I am doing, I'll do it."

In the Message Translation, trust is the foundation. The Message emphasizes "trust" as the cornerstone of the believer's relationship with Jesus. This trust empowers believers to engage in the works of Christ, suggesting that prayer is an expression of this trust and reliance on His power.

Greater Works
The phrase "even greater things" is framed positively, indicating that believers will continue and expand upon Jesus 'mission. The New Covenant empowers believers to engage in transformative work that extends beyond the physical to spiritual realms.

These Requests Aligned with Christ's Purpose
The phrase "along the lines of who I am and what I am doing" stresses the importance of aligning our requests with

Christ's character and mission. This perspective invites believers to consider the broader context of their prayers, ensuring that they reflect the heart of God.

It makes the character of the Father more visible. The Message translation clarifies that the purpose of answered prayer is to reveal the Father's character. This aligns with the New Covenant reality that our prayers should reflect God's glory, showcasing His love and power in the world. The New Covenant reality of prayer, as articulated in **John 14:12-14**, emphasizes a deep, trusting relationship with Jesus that empowers believers to pray with authority and purpose. By praying in His name, believers access the power of Christ's mission, ensuring that their requests align with God's will and ultimately glorify Him. This perspective transforms prayer from a routine duty into a dynamic partnership with God, where believers actively participate in His redemptive work. Through this lens, prayer becomes a powerful tool for demonstrating faith, reflecting God's character, and advancing His kingdom on earth.

Chapter 9

The Holy Spirit is the Promise of the New Covenant.

Luke 24:44 *And he said unto them, These are the words which I spake unto you, while I was yet with you, that all things must be fulfilled, which were written in the law of Moses, and in the prophets, and in the psalms, concerning me.*

Luke 24:45 *Then opened he their understanding, that they might understand the scriptures,*

Luke 24:46 *And said unto them, Thus it is written, and thus it behoved Christ to suffer, and to rise from the dead the third day:*

Luke 24:47 *And that repentance and remission of sins should be preached in his name among all nations, beginning at Jerusalem.*

Luke 24:48 *And ye are witnesses of these things.*

Luke 24:49 *And, behold, I send the promise of my Father upon you: but tarry ye in the city of Jerusalem, until ye be endued with power from on high.*

The Promise of the New Covenant: The Holy Spirit in Luke 24:44-49

The New Covenant represents a transformative shift in God's relationship with humanity, ushering in an era defined by grace, redemption, and the indwelling presence of the Holy Spirit. **In Luke 24:44-49**, we find Jesus affirming this new reality, providing profound insight into the role of the Holy Spirit as a promise and a gift to His followers. This passage not only underscores the significance of the resurrection but also establishes the foundation for the Church's mission, empowered by the Holy Spirit.

The Gospel of Luke culminates in a climactic moment where the resurrected Christ appears to His disciples. This scene is set in a post-resurrection context, where disbelief and confusion still loom among the disciples. They have witnessed the crucifixion and the empty tomb, yet they struggle to comprehend the reality of the resurrection. Jesus, in His mercy, seeks to clarify their understanding and instill in them the hope of the Holy Spirit's coming.

In verses 44-46, Jesus begins by reminding His disciples of the Scriptures that foretell His suffering, death, and resurrection. He states, *"These are my words that I spoke to you while I was still with you, that everything written about me in the Law of Moses and the Prophets and the Psalms must be fulfilled."* This declaration emphasizes that the events they have witnessed are not random but part of God's divine plan, meticulously foretold through the prophetic writings.

Jesus connects His mission to the broader narrative of Scripture, revealing that His life, death, and resurrection are the fulfillment of God's promises. This linkage is crucial; it grounds the disciples in the faithfulness of God's word and prepares them for the next phase of their journey—the empowerment of the Holy Spirit.

In verse 47, Jesus articulates the core of the new covenant: *"And that repentance for the forgiveness of sins should be proclaimed in his name to all nations, beginning from Jerusalem."* Here, we see the commissioning of the disciples. They are called to proclaim the good news of repentance and forgiveness, a message that is deeply rooted in the new covenant's tenets.

The Holy Spirit's role becomes paramount in this mission. The disciples, who once cowered in fear, are to be transformed into bold proclaimers of the Gospel. The promise of the Holy Spirit is essential for this transformation, as it empowers them to carry out the commission that transcends cultural and geographical boundaries.

In verse 49, Jesus states, *"And behold, I am sending the promise of my Father upon you. But stay in the city until you are clothed with power from on high."* The promise of the Father refers to the Holy Spirit, who is to come upon them and empower their ministry. This promise signifies a new reality: God's presence will no longer dwell in the temple alone but will inhabit the hearts of believers.

The phrase "clothed with power from on high" evokes imagery of divine enablement. Just as clothing signifies an identity and a role, the Holy Spirit will envelop the disciples, marking them as agents of God's kingdom. This empowerment is essential for the daunting task ahead, equipping them with boldness, wisdom, and spiritual gifts to carry forth the Gospel.

The New Covenant Reality promise of the Holy Spirit encapsulates the essence of the new covenant: an intimate relationship with God, mediated by the Spirit. Unlike the old covenant, which was characterized by laws written on stone, the new covenant brings about a transformation of the heart. Through the Holy Spirit, believers are given the ability to live out God's commands, fostering a community marked by love, grace, and unity.

As the disciples await the coming of the Holy Spirit, they enter a period of anticipation and preparation. This waiting is not passive; it is a time of prayer, reflection, and unity, setting the stage for the outpouring of the Spirit at Pentecost. This pivotal moment transforms their understanding of mission and community, empowering them to live out the implications of the resurrection.

The Promise in Acts 1:4-8

The narrative continues in **Acts 1:4-8**, where the connection between the resurrection, the promise of the Holy Spirit, and the mission of the Church becomes even clearer. In this passage, Jesus commands His disciples to remain in Jerusalem until they receive the Holy Spirit. He says, *"Do not depart from Jerusalem, but wait for the promise of the Father, which you heard from me."*

Waiting for the Promise

The directive to wait is significant. It emphasizes the necessity of divine empowerment before embarking on their mission. The disciples are instructed to stay put, signifying that their work is not to be done in their own strength but through the power that the Holy Spirit will provide. This period of waiting fosters unity and dependence on God, highlighting the importance of spiritual preparation.

The Role of the Holy Spirit

In verse 5, Jesus elaborates on the Holy Spirit's role, stating, *"For John baptized with water, but you will be baptized with the Holy Spirit not many days from now."* This baptism in the Holy Spirit signifies a profound transformation, a complete immersion in God's presence and power. The distinction between water baptism and Spirit baptism points to the new covenant's depth, where believers are not only cleansed but also empowered to live out their faith dynamically.

The Mission Ahead

As the passage unfolds, verse 8 encapsulates the mission: *"But you will receive power when the Holy Spirit has come upon you, and you will be my witnesses in Jerusalem and in all Judea and Samaria, and to the end of the earth."* Here, Jesus outlines the scope of their mission, emphasizing that the Holy Spirit will enable them to be witnesses, starting from Jerusalem and extending to the farthest reaches of the earth.

This promise of power is crucial; it signifies that the disciples are not merely sent out as individuals but as a community empowered by the Spirit. The Holy Spirit transforms their identity and purpose, equipping them to bear witness to the resurrection and the message of salvation.

The Assurance of the Promise in Acts 2:33-39

The promise of the Holy Spirit is further affirmed in **Acts 2:33-39** during Peter's Pentecost sermon. Here, Peter explains that the outpouring of the Holy Spirit which the disciples have just experienced is a direct fulfillment of the promise made by Jesus. He boldly declares that Jesus, exalted at the right hand of God, has poured out the Spirit, confirming that this gift is not limited to the apostles alone.

In verse 39, Peter states, *"For the promise is for you and for your children and for all who are far off, everyone whom the Lord our God calls to himself."* This declaration broadens the scope of the promise, emphasizing that the gift of the Holy Spirit is available to future generations and all who respond to God's call.

This inclusivity highlights the enduring nature of God's covenant relationship. It reassures believers that the empowering presence of the Holy Spirit is accessible to all— young and old—who seek to follow Christ. The promise is not confined to the initial disciples but extends through time, inviting every believer into a life empowered by the Spirit.

The Implications of Galatians 3:13-2
To further understand the significance of the Holy Spirit in the context of the New Covenant, we turn to **Galatians 3:13-29**. In this passage, the Apostle Paul articulates the implications of the Law, grace, and the promise received through faith in Christ.

Redemption from the Curse of the Law
Paul begins in verse 13 by stating, *"Christ redeemed us from the curse of the law by becoming a curse for us."* Here, he emphasizes that through Christ's sacrificial death,

believers are liberated from the demands of the Law, which could never bring salvation. This act of redemption is central to the New Covenant, marking a shift from a system of works to one of grace.

The Promise of the Spirit

In verses 14-15, Paul explains that the blessing of Abraham comes to the Gentiles through faith in Jesus Christ, and that we might receive the promised Spirit through faith. This connects back to the promise of the Holy Spirit as a gift not only for the Jewish believers but for all who believe. The Holy Spirit becomes the seal of this new covenant, a mark of belonging to God's family.

Unity in Christ

Paul continues in verses 26-28, stating, *"For in Christ Jesus you are all sons of God, through faith. For as many of you as were baptized into Christ have put on Christ."* This declaration highlights the radical inclusivity of the New Covenant. In Christ, distinctions that often divide—such as Jew or Gentile, slave or free, male or female—are transcended. All believers are united as children of God, empowered by the same Spirit.

Heirs of the Promise

Finally, in verse 29, Paul concludes with a powerful affirmation: *"And if you are Christ's, then you are Abraham's offspring, heirs according to promise."* This inheritance signifies that all believers have access to the promises of God, including the gift of the Holy Spirit. Each believer becomes a participant in the covenant promises, further underscoring the idea that the Holy Spirit is a gift for all generations.

In Luke 24:44-49, Acts 1:4-8, Acts 2:33-39, and **Galatians 3:13-29**, we witness the profound transition from the earthly ministry of Jesus to the empowered mission of the Church. The promise of the Holy Spirit is central to this new covenant reality, enabling believers to share the message of repentance and forgiveness with the world. As we reflect on these passages, we are reminded that the Holy Spirit continues to be our guide and empowerer, shaping our lives and our mission as we engage with the world, embodying the transformative love of Christ. The New Covenant, sealed by the Holy Spirit, invites us into a dynamic relationship with God, where we are equipped to participate in His redemptive work across generations, ensuring that the promise of the Spirit is a gift for us, our children, and all who come to faith in Christ. Through the Holy Spirit, we are united as heirs of God's promises, called to live out our faith empowered by His presence.

What is in the New Covenant Reality for our lives?

The reality of salvation is in the covenant.
The reality of peace is in the covenant.
The reality of joy is in the covenant.
The reality of healing is in the covenant.
The reality of prosperity is in the covenant.
The reality of long life is in the covenant.

This is all part of the price that Jesus paid for us when he went to the cross and he spilled his blood to fulfill the promises and to establish a new covenant reality for his children, and scripture became a reality by faith in the Son of God. The Holy Spirit is our empowerment to obtain all that God had promised through the scripture and bring them into a reality by faith. We must continue to be people of Faith so that we will continue to walk by the spirit of God and see our covenant become a reality now.

Hebrews 11:1 *Now faith is the substance of things hoped for, the evidence of things not seen.*

Let me end with this. When we walk in a New Covenant Reality in our Christian lives, we will understand that everything becomes a reality in **Faith Now!** We obtain every promise of God by the ability of the Holy Spirit "in the now", waiting for the manifestation of what we have already received by Faith.